STEVIE RAY VAUGHAN

Ain't Gone 'n' Give Up on Love

Written by Stevie Ray Vaughan

C Version

Book & Audio for B♭, E♭, Bass Clef and C instruments

PLAY 8 SONGS WITH A PROFESSIONAL BAND

HOW TO USE THE AUDIO:

Each song has multiple tracks:

1) Full Stereo Mix
All recorded instruments are present on this track.

2) Minus Guitar Mix

3) Minus Bass Mix

4) Minus Keyboard Mix

5) Minus Drums Mix

Speed • Pitch • Balance • Loop

To access audio visit:
www.halleonard.com/mylibrary

Enter Code
6974-1303-7785-1080

ISBN 978-1-4234-9989-3

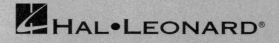

Visit Hal Leonard Online at
www.halleonard.com

Contact Us:
Hal Leonard
7777 West Bluemound Road
Milwaukee, WI 53213
Email: info@halleonard.com

In Europe contact:
Hal Leonard Europe Limited
42 Wigmore Street
Marylebone, London, W1U 2RN
Email: info@halleonardeurope.com

In Australia contact:
Hal Leonard Australia Pty. Ltd.
4 Lentara Court
Cheltenham, Victoria, 3192 Australia
Email: info@halleonard.com.au

AH, EV - 'RY TEAR THAT I'VE CRIED _____

ON - LY WASHED A - WAY THE FEAR IN - SIDE. _ NOW I, _____ I AIN'T GONE 'N' GIVE UP ON _____

BRIDGE

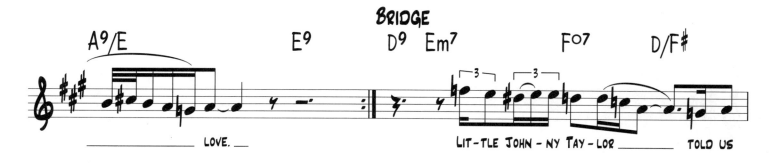

_____ LOVE. _ LIT - TLE JOHN - NY TAY - LOR _____ TOLD US

SO _ LONG _ A - GO _____ ALL A - BOUT _ THE MID - NIGHT CRY - IN',

WHOA, _ 'N' THAT YOU BEEN LY - IN'. WHAT A - BOUT THE PRICE ___ THAT WILL. _

OH, _ SURE - LY BE PAID _____ 'CAUSE THEY GAVE UP ON LOVE?

LOVE WILL HAVE ITS DAY. _____ I AIN'T GIV-IN' UP ON _____

SOLOS

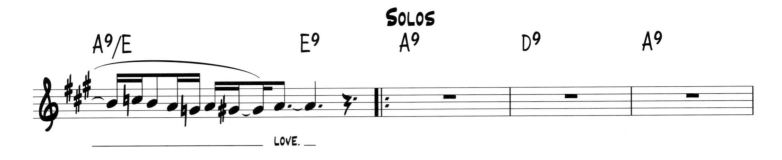

_____ LOVE. __

OUTRO-VERSE

3. I AIN'T GON' GIVE UP ON _____ LOVE. LOVE _____ WON'T GIVE UP

ON _____ ME. _____

I ___ AIN'T GONE 'N' GIVE UP ON ___ LOVE. ___

___ LOVE. ___ WON'T GIVE, AH, UP ON ___ ME. ___ AH, HA. ___

___ EV - 'RY TIME ___ I CRY, ___

LORD, ___ JUST, AH, WON'T 'N' LET ___ ME, ___ME ___ BE.

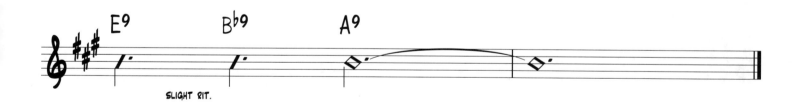

SLIGHT RIT.

ADDITIONAL LYRICS

2. EV'RY BEAT OF MY HEART POUNDS WITH JOY 'N' NOT PAIN.
   EV'RY BEAT OF MY HEART POUNDS WITH JOY 'N' BURNIN' PAIN.
   'CAUSE ALL THOSE PAINFUL MEMORIES ONLY BROUGHT ME TO MY KNEES.
   I WAS JUST GIVIN' UP ON LOVE.

Couldn't Stand the Weather

Written by Stevie Ray Vaughan

C Version

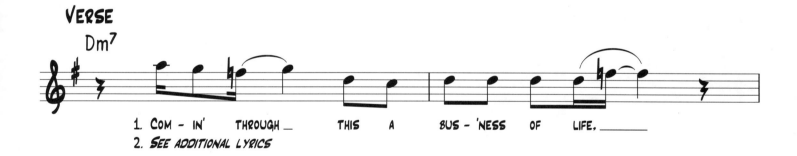

1. COM - IN' THROUGH __ THIS A BUS - 'NESS OF LIFE, _____
2. *SEE ADDITIONAL LYRICS*

RARE - LY TIME ___ IF I'M NEED - ED TO. _____

AIN'T SO FUN - NY WHEN THINGS ____ AIN'T FEEL - IN' RIGHT, __

THEN DAD-DY'S HAND ___ HELPS TO SEE ME THROUGH. ___

SWEET AS SUG-AR, LOVE WON'T ___ WASH A-WAY. ___ RAIN OR SHINE, IT'S AL-

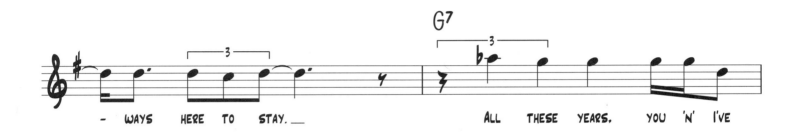

- WAYS HERE TO STAY. ___ ALL THESE YEARS, YOU 'N' I'VE

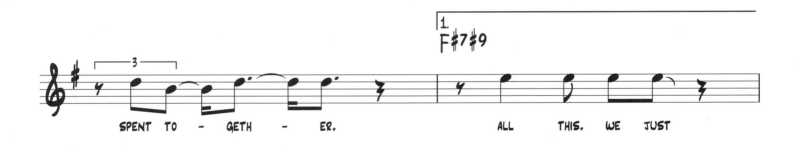

SPENT TO-GETH-ER, ALL THIS, WE JUST

COULD-N'T STAND THE WEATH-ER. UN-DER-STAND, ___ IT'S

TIME TO GET R - READ-Y FOR THE STORM. ___

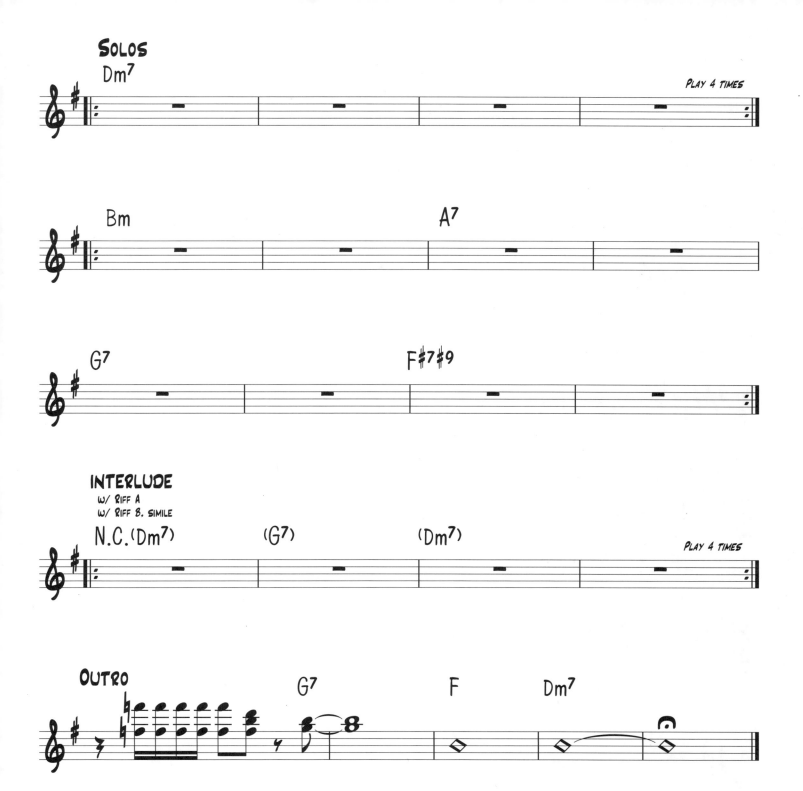

ADDITIONAL LYRICS

2. Like a train that stops at ev'ry station,
   We all deal with trials and tribulations.
   Fear hangs the fellow that ties up his years,
   Entangled in yellow and cries all his tears.
   Changes come before we can go.
   Learn to see them before we're too old.
   Don't just take me for tryin' to be heavy.
   Understand, it's time to get ready for the storm.

CROSSFIRE

WORDS AND MUSIC BY BILL CARTER, RUTH ELLSWORTH,
REESE WYNANS, TOMMY SHANNON AND CHRIS LAYTON

C VERSION

CAUGHT IN ___ THE CROSS - FIRE.

STRAND - ED, _____
2. I AM STRAND - ED, _____
3. WE GOT STRAND - ED, _____

BRIDGE
G7

CAUGHT IN THE CROSS - FIRE.

I NEED SOME

A7

G7

A7

KIND OF KIND-NESS, ___ SOME KIND OF SYM-PA- THY. ___ OH, NO, ___ WE'RE

N.C.(E7)

STRAND - ED, ___ CAUGHT IN THE CROSS - FIRE.

SOLOS
E7

PLAY 4 TIMES

G7

A7

G7

A7

E

D.S. AL CODA

CAUGHT IN THE CROSS-

- FIRE.   WE GOT STRAND - ED, _____

CAUGHT IN THE CROSS - FIRE.   STRAND - ED, _____

CAUGHT IN ____ THE CROSS - FIRE.

OUTRO-SOLO

E7

PLAY 7 TIMES

N.C.   E7#9

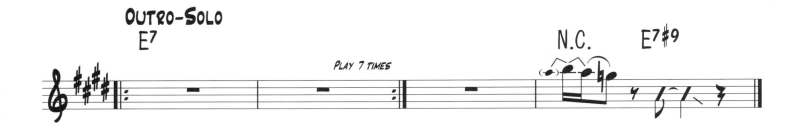

ADDITIONAL LYRICS

2. TOOTH FOR TOOTH, EYE FOR AN EYE,
   SELL YOUR SOUL JUST TO BUY, BUY, BUY.
   BEGGIN' A DOLLAR, STEAL-IN' A DIME,
   COME ON, CAN'T CHA SEE THAT I,...

3. SAVE THE STRONG, LOSE THE WEAK,
   NEVER TURNING THE OTHER CHEEK.
   TRUST NOBODY, DON'T BE NO FOOL.
   WHATEVER HAPPENED TO THE GOLDEN RULE?

Honey Bee

Written by Stevie Ray Vaughan

C Version

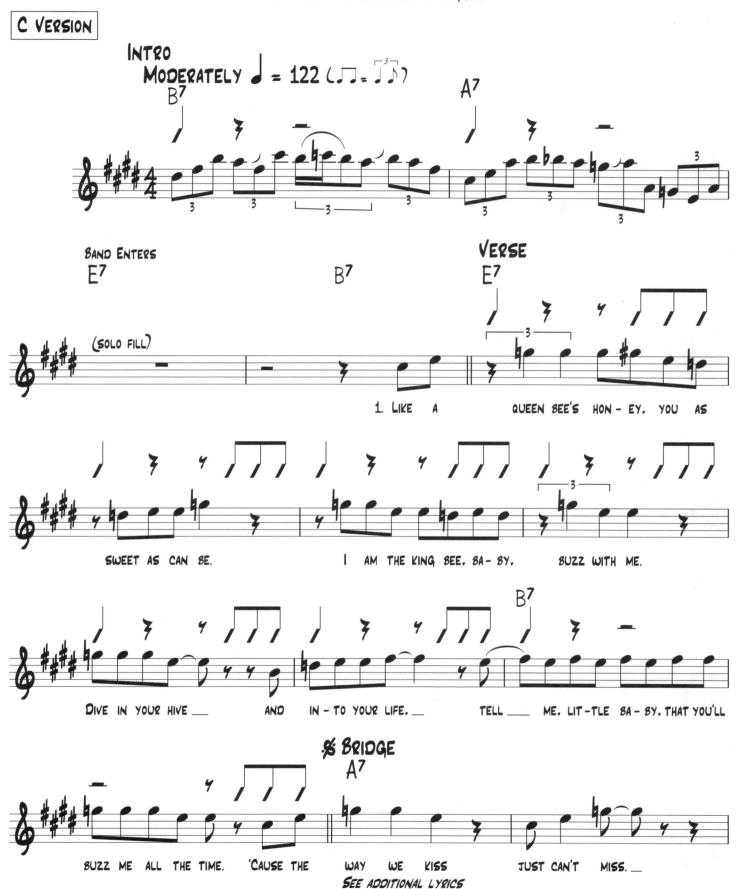

See additional lyrics

Don't make me wait to feel your warm em - brace.

Each and ev - 'ry time that we get the chance,__ C -

B7   To Coda ⊕   E7

'mon, lit - tle ba - by, let's, ah, make some ro - mance.

SOLO
E7

A7   E7

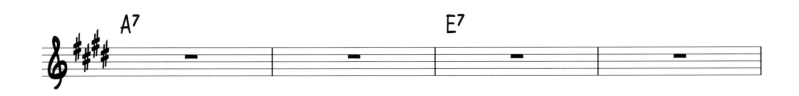

B7   A7   E7

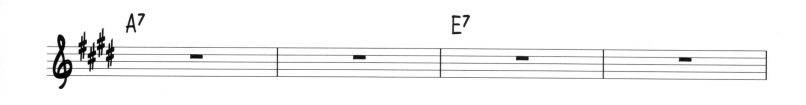

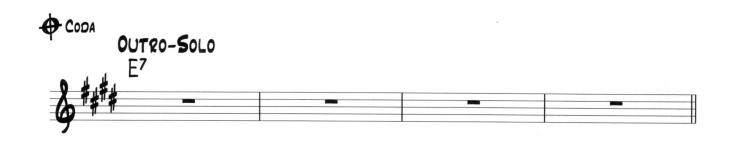

ADDITIONAL LYRICS

BRIDGE: YEAH, YOU REALLY GROOVE ME, BABY, WHEN YOU MOVE YOUR HIPS.
SHAKE IT ALL AROUND, IT TAKES ME POUND FOR POUND.
I WANT YOU ALL THE TIME JUST BECAUSE,
YOU KNOW YOU REALLY HAVE GIVE ME A BUZZ.

Empty Arms

Written by Stevie Ray Vaughan

C Version

INTRO
Moderately fast ♩ = 142

BAND ENTERS

INTRO/SOLO

1. YOU'RE GON - NA MISS ___

$ VERSE

C

___ ME, LIT - TLE BA - BY, THE DAY THAT I'M GONE. ___

2., - 5. SEE ADDITIONAL LYRICS

You're gon-na miss ___ me, lit-tle dar - lin',

the day that I'm gone. ___ 'Cause I'm

5TH TIME, TO CODA

Leav-in' in the morn - in', won't be back at all. ___

1., 4.   2.   3.

2. You have run ___   3. You can try ___
5. You can try ___

Solos

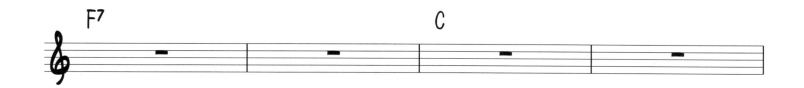

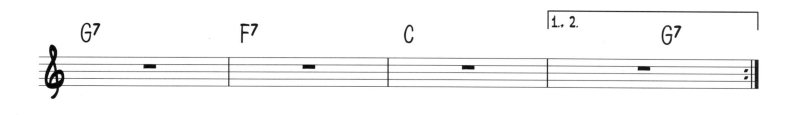

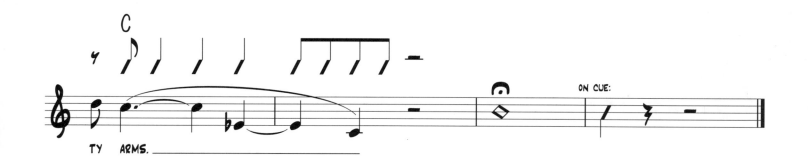

ADDITIONAL LYRICS

2., 4. YOU HAVE RUN ME RAGGED, BABY.
IT'S YOUR OWN FAULT YOU'RE ON YOUR OWN.
YOU HAVE RUN ME RAGGED, DARLIN'.
IT'S YOUR OWN FAULT YOU'RE ON YOUR OWN.
YOU DIDN'T WANT ME TO WAIT, BABY,
TILL YOUR OTHER MAN WAS GONE.

3., 5. YOU CAN TRY TO GE ME BACK, BABY,
WITH ALL YOUR TRICKS AND CHARMS.
YOU CAN TRY TO GET ME BACK, BABY,
WITH ALL YOUR TRICKS AND CHARMS.
BUT WHEN ALL YOUR GAMES ARE OVER,
YOU'LL BE LEFT WITH EMPTY ARMS.

Rude Mood

Written by Stevie Ray Vaughan

C Version

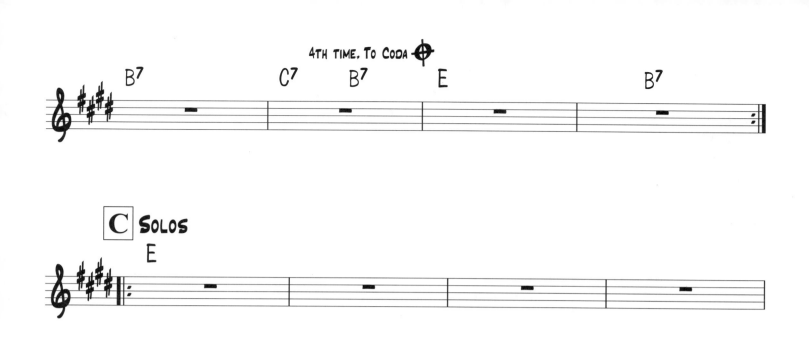

SCUTTLE BUTTIN'

Written by Stevie Ray Vaughan

C Version

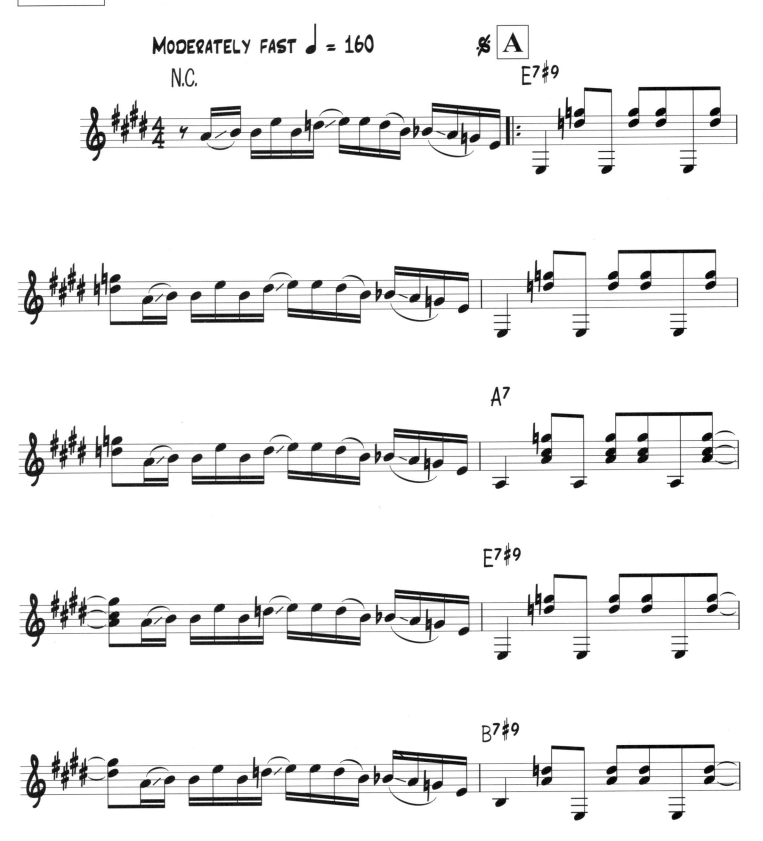

Love Struck Baby

Written by Stevie Ray Vaughan

C Version

LOVE YOU, BA - BY, AN' I KNOW JUST WHAT TO DO. ____

%̸ VERSE

1. I ____ STILL RE-MEM-BER, AN' LET IT BE SAID, ____ THE
2., 3. *SEE ADDITIONAL LYRICS*

WAY YOU MAKE ME FEEL, IT'LL TAKE A FOOL TO FOR-GET. I SWORE A TON OF BRICKS HAD HIT ME

1.

IN THE HEAD, __ AN' WHAT YOU DO, LIT-TLE BA-BY, AIN'T O - VER IT YET.

2., 3. **CHORUS**

____ YOUR MAN? I'M A LOVE STRUCK, BA-BY. YEAH, I'M A

LOVE STRUCK, BA-BY. YOU GOT ME LOVE STRUCK, BA-BY,

AND   I   KNOW   JUST   WHAT   TO   DO. ____

SOLOS

ADDITIONAL LYRICS

2. EVERYTIME I SEE YOU, MAKE ME FEEL SO FINE.
   HEART BEATIN' CRAZY, MY BLOOD RUNNIN' WILD.
   LOVIN' MAKES ME FEEL LIKE A MIGHTY, MIGHTY MAN.
   LOVE ME, BABY, AIN'T I YOUR MAN?

3. SPARKS START FLYIN' EVERYTIME WE MEET.
   LET ME TELL YOU, BABY, YOU KNOCK ME OFF MY FEET.
   YOUR KISSES TRIP ME UP AND THEY'RE JUST DOG GONE SWEET.
   DON'T YOU KNOW, BABY, YOU KNOCK ME OFF MY FEET?

CROSSFIRE

WORDS AND MUSIC BY BILL CARTER, RUTH ELLSWORTH, REESE WYNANS, TOMMY SHANNON AND CHRIS LAYTON

Bb VERSION

CAUGHT IN ___ THE CROSS - FIRE.   STRAND - ED. _____
{ 2. I AM STRAND - ED. _____ }
{ 3. WE GOT STRAND - ED. _____ }

BRIDGE
A⁷

CAUGHT IN THE CROSS - FIRE.   I NEED SOME

B⁷   A⁷   B⁷

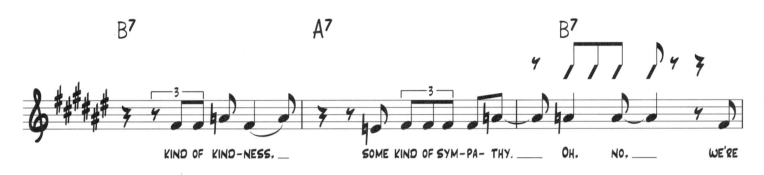

KIND OF KIND - NESS. __   SOME KIND OF SYM - PA - THY. ___ OH. NO. ___   WE'RE

N.C.(F♯⁷)

STRAND - ED. ___   CAUGHT IN THE CROSS - FIRE.

SOLOS
F♯⁷   PLAY 4 TIMES   A⁷

B⁷   A⁷   B⁷   F♯

CAUGHT IN THE CROSS-

- FIRE.   WE GOT STRAND - ED, _____

CAUGHT IN THE CROSS - FIRE.   STRAND - ED, _____

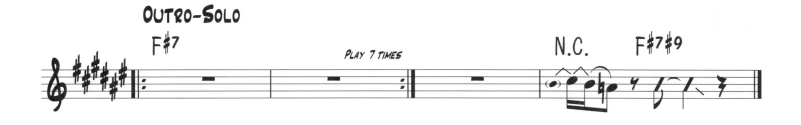

CAUGHT IN _____ THE CROSS - FIRE.

OUTRO-SOLO

Additional Lyrics

2. Tooth for tooth, eye for an eye,
   Sell your soul just to buy, buy, buy.
   Beggin' a dollar, steal-in' a dime,
   Come on, can't cha see that I,...

3. Save the strong, lose the weak,
   Never turning the other cheek.
   Trust nobody, don't be no fool.
   Whatever happened to the golden rule?

Ain't Gone 'n' Give Up on Love

Written by Stevie Ray Vaughan

Bb Version

1. I ain't gon' give up on __ love. __
2. See additional lyrics

Me.   I, __

I ain't gone 'n' give up on __ love. __   Love _____ ain't gon' give up on __

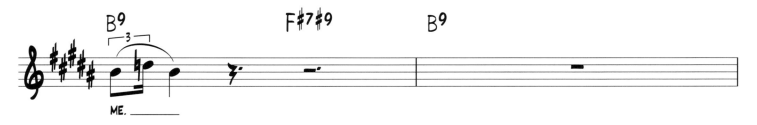

Me. __

Ah, ev-'ry tear that I've cried _____

On-ly washed a-way the fear in - side. _ Now I, _____ I ain't gone 'n' give up on _____

_____ Love. _ Lit-tle John-ny Tay-lor _____ told us

So _ long _ a - go _____ All a-bout _ the mid-night cry - in',

Whoa, _ 'n' that you been ly-in'. What a-bout the price _____ that will, _

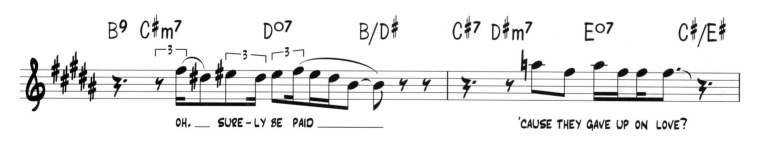

Oh, _ sure-ly be paid _____ 'cause they gave up on love?

Love will _ have its day. _____ I ain't giv-in' up on ___

SOLOS

_____ love. _____

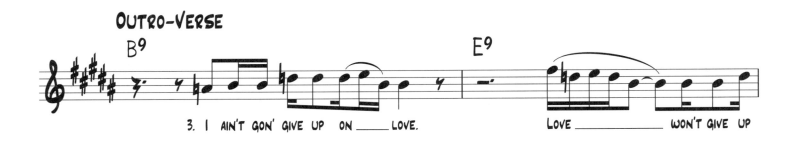

OUTRO-VERSE

3. I ain't gon' give up on __ love. Love _____ won't give up

on __ me. _____

I ___ AIN'T GONE 'N' GIVE UP ON ___ LOVE. ___

___ LOVE, ___ WON'T GIVE, AH, UP ON ___ ME, ___ AH, HA. ___

___ EV - 'RY TIME ___ I CRY, ___

LORD, ___ JUST, AH, WON'T 'N' LET ___ ME, ___ ME ___ BE. ___

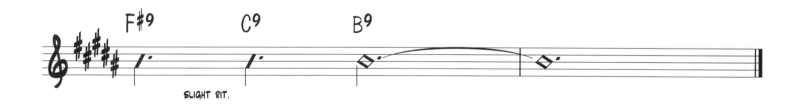

SLIGHT RIT.

ADDITIONAL LYRICS

2. EV'RY BEAT OF MY HEART POUNDS WITH JOY 'N' NOT PAIN.
   EV'RY BEAT OF MY HEART POUNDS WITH JOY 'N' BURNIN' PAIN.
   'CAUSE ALL THOSE PAINFUL MEMORIES ONLY BROUGHT ME TO MY KNEES.
   I WAS JUST GIVIN' UP ON LOVE.

Couldn't Stand the Weather

Written by Stevie Ray Vaughan

Bb Version

w/ RIFF A
w/ RIFF B, SIMILE

(Em7)   (A7)   (Em7)

(A7)   (Em7)

VERSE
Em7

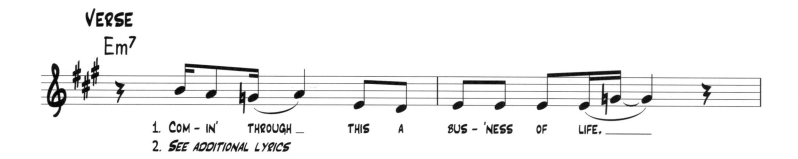

1. COM - IN' THROUGH ___ THIS A BUS - 'NESS OF LIFE, _____
2. *SEE ADDITIONAL LYRICS*

RARE - LY TIME ___ IF I'M NEED - ED TO. _____

AIN'T SO FUN - NY WHEN THINGS ___ AIN'T FEEL - IN' RIGHT, _

THEN DAD-DY'S HAND ___ HELPS TO SEE ME THROUGH. ___

SWEET AS SUG-AR, LOVE WON'T ____ WASH A-WAY. ___ RAIN OR SHINE, IT'S AL -

- WAYS HERE TO STAY. ___ ALL THESE YEARS, YOU 'N' I'VE

SPENT TO - GETH - ER, ALL THIS, WE JUST

COULD - N'T STAND THE WEATH - ER. UN - DER - STAND, ___ IT'S

TIME TO GET R - READ - Y FOR THE STORM. ____

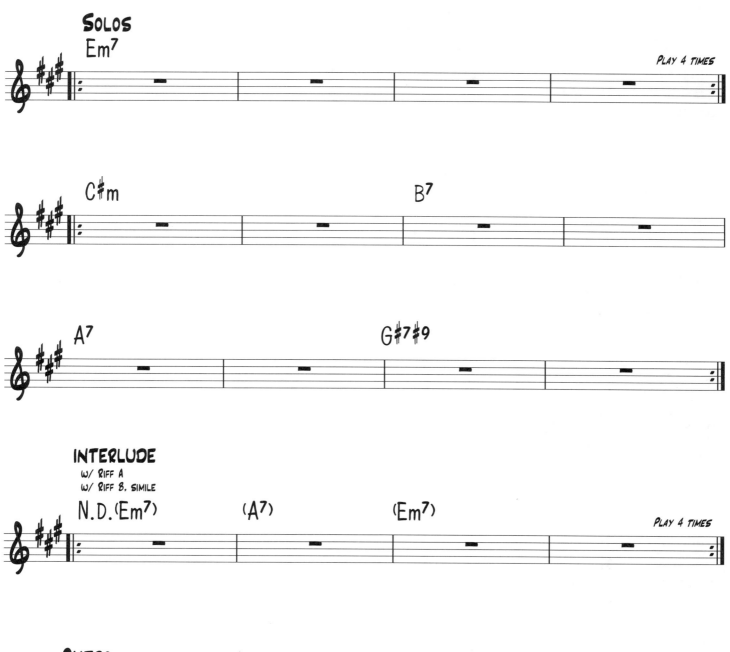

Additional Lyrics

2. Like a train that stops at ev'ry station,
   We all deal with trials and tribulations.
   Fear hangs the fellow that ties up his years,
   Entangled in yellow and cries all his tears.
   Changes come before we can go.
   Learn to see them before we're too old.
   Don't just take me for tryin' to be heavy.
   Understand, it's time to get ready for the storm.

Empty Arms

Written by Stevie Ray Vaughan

Bb Version

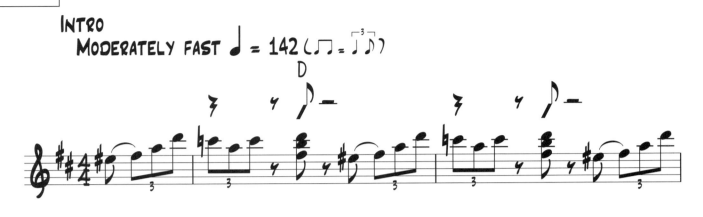

G7   D9

                      A7   G7

D9   A7

1. YOU'RE GON - NA MISS __

VERSE

D

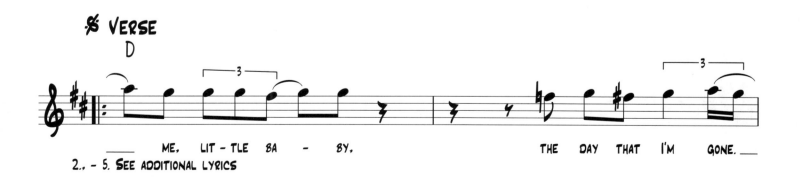

__ ME, LIT - TLE BA — BY,   THE DAY THAT I'M GONE. __

2., - 5. SEE ADDITIONAL LYRICS

YOU'RE GON-NA MISS ___ ME, LIT-TLE DAR - LIN',

THE DAY THAT I'M GONE. _____ 'CAUSE I'M

5TH TIME, TO CODA ✛

LEAV-IN' IN THE MORN - IN', WON'T BE BACK AT ALL. _____

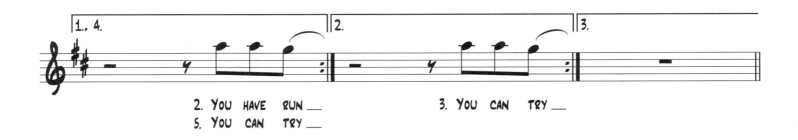

2. YOU HAVE RUN ___   3. YOU CAN TRY ___
5. YOU CAN TRY ___

SOLOS

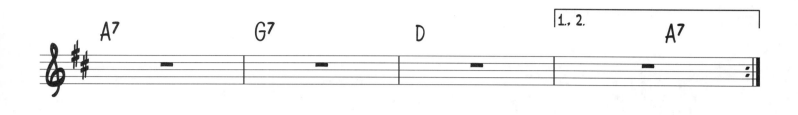

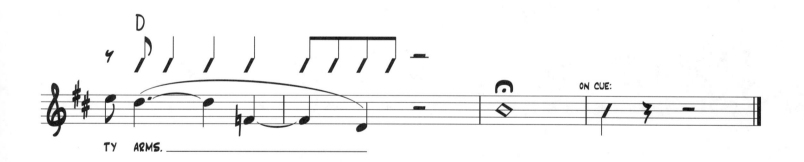

Additional Lyrics

2., 4. You have run me ragged, baby.
It's your own fault you're on your own.
You have run me ragged, darlin'.
It's your own fault you're on your own.
You didn't want me to wait, baby,
Till your other man was gone.

3., 5. You can try to ge me back, baby,
With all your tricks and charms.
You can try to get me back, baby,
With all your tricks and charms.
But when all your games are over,
You'll be left with empty arms.

Honey Bee

Written by Stevie Ray Vaughan

Bb Version

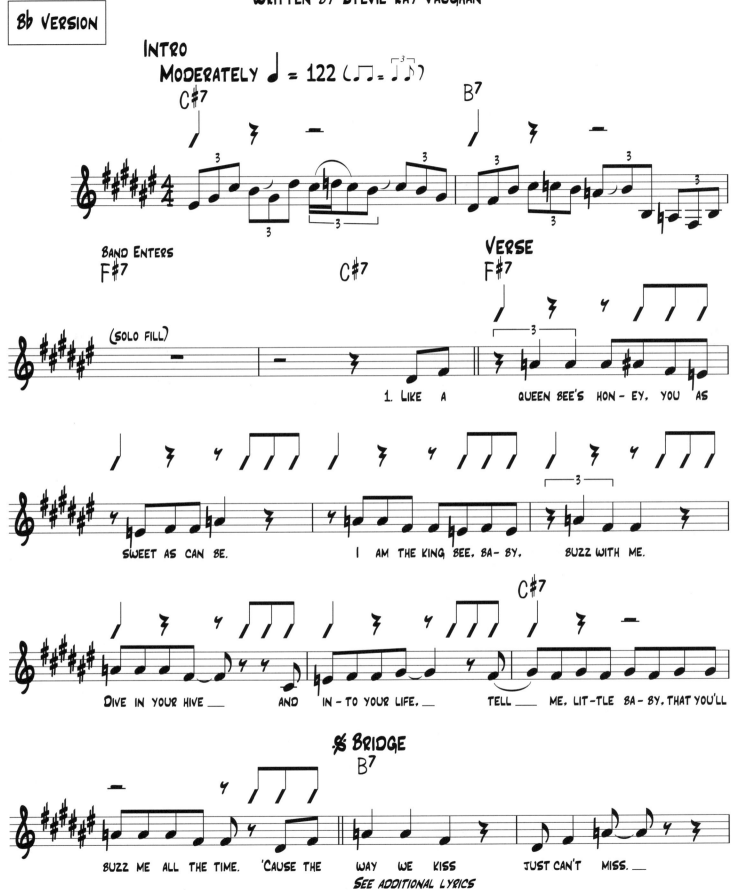

INTRO
Moderately ♩ = 122

Band Enters

Verse

1. Like a queen bee's hon-ey, you as sweet as can be. I am the king bee, ba-by, buzz with me. Dive in your hive ___ and in-to your life, ___ tell ___ me, lit-tle ba-by, that you'll

Bridge

Buzz me all the time. 'Cause the way we kiss just can't miss. ___

See additional lyrics

Don't make me wait to feel your warm em - brace.

Each and ev - 'ry time that we get the chance, ___ C -

To Coda

'mon, lit - tle ba - by, let's, ah, make some ro - mance.

Solo

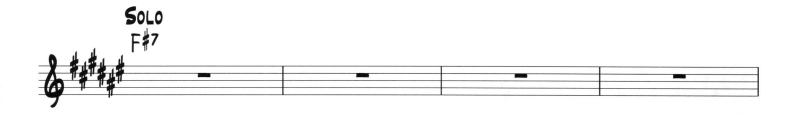

D.S. AL CODA

YEAH, YOU

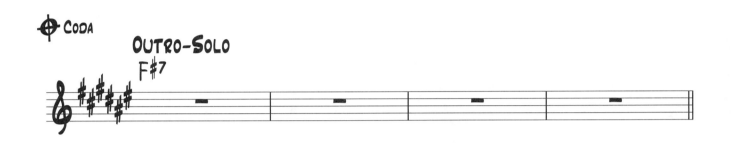

OUTRO-SOLO

ADDITIONAL LYRICS

BRIDGE: YEAH, YOU REALLY GROOVE ME, BABY, WHEN YOU MOVE YOUR HIPS.
SHAKE IT ALL AROUND, IT TAKES ME POUND FOR POUND.
I WANT YOU ALL THE TIME JUST BECAUSE,
YOU KNOW YOU REALLY HAVE GIVE ME A BUZZ.

Love Struck Baby

Written by Stevie Ray Vaughan

Bb Version

Intro
Moderately fast ♩ = 170

Well, I'm a

Chorus

LOVE STRUCK, BA - BY, I ____ MUST CON - FESS. ____ Life ____ WITH - OUT YOU, DAR - LING'S, JUST A

SOL - ID MESS. ____ THINK - IN' 'BOUT YOU, BA - BY, GIVE ME SUCH A THRILL, ____ I GOT - TA

HAVE YOU, MM, BA - BY, CAN'T ____ GET MY FILL. ____ I ____

F#7   B7

LOVE YOU, BA - BY, AN' I KNOW JUST WHAT TO DO. ____

𝄋 VERSE

F#7   E7

1. I ____ STILL RE - MEM - BER, AN' LET IT BE SAID, ___ THE
2., 3. *See additional lyrics*

B7   E7

WAY YOU MAKE ME FEEL, IT'LL TAKE A FOOL TO FOR - GET. I SWORE A TON OF BRICKS HAD HIT ME

F#7   1.

IN THE HEAD, ___ AN' WHAT YOU DO, LIT - TLE BA - BY, AIN'T O - VER IT YET.

2., 3.   CHORUS
B7

____ YOUR MAN? I'M A LOVE STRUCK, BA - BY.   YEAH, I'M A

E7   B7

LOVE STRUCK, BA - BY.   YOU GOT ME LOVE STRUCK, BA - BY,

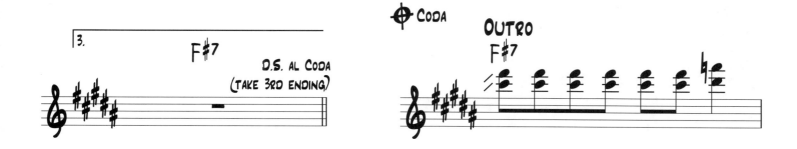

Additional Lyrics

2. Everytime I see you, make me feel so fine.
   Heart beatin' crazy, my blood runnin' wild.
   Lovin' makes me feel like a mighty, mighty man.
   Love me, baby, ain't I your man?

3. Sparks start flyin' everytime we meet.
   Let me tell you, baby, you knock me off my feet.
   Your kisses trip me up and they're just dog gone sweet.
   Don't you know, baby, you knock me off my feet?

Rude Mood

Written by Stevie Ray Vaughan

8b Version

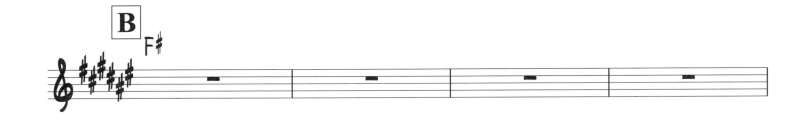

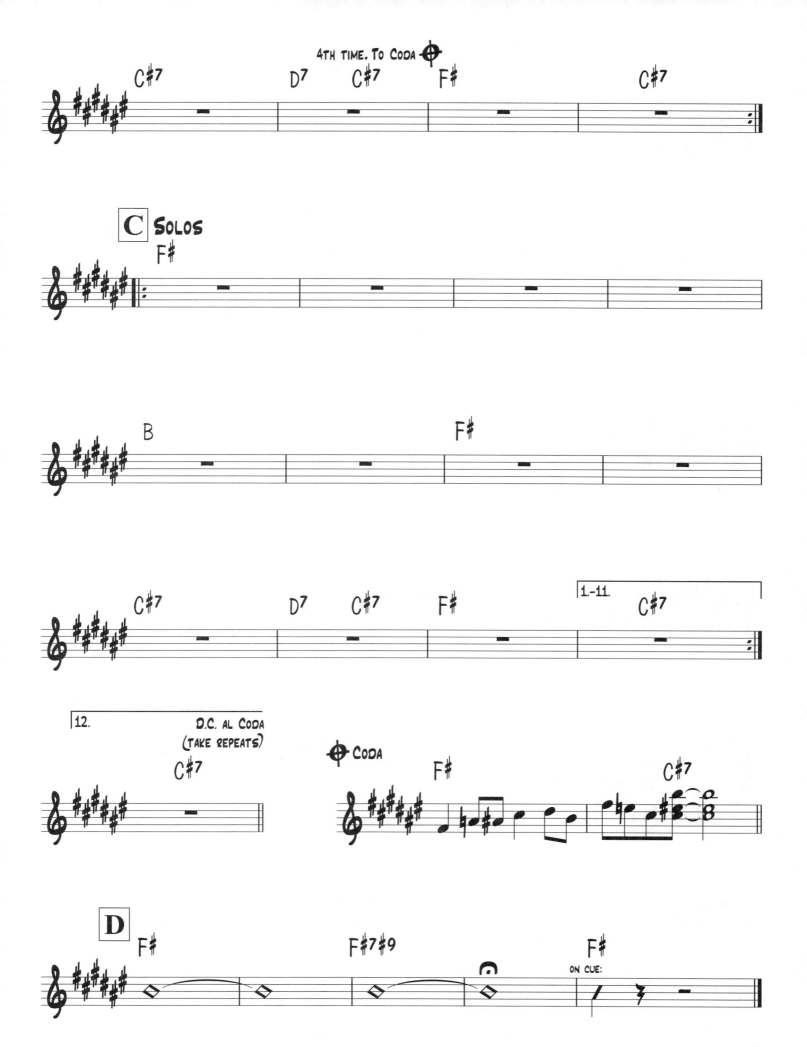

Scuttle Buttin'

Written by Stevie Ray Vaughan

Bb Version

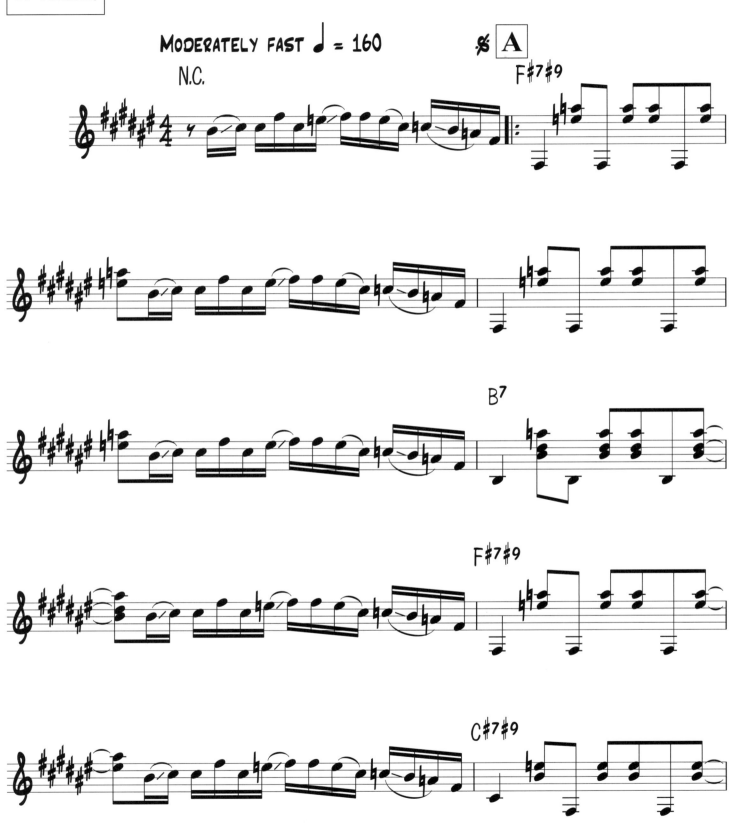

Ain't Gone 'N' Give Up on Love

Written by Stevie Ray Vaughan

Eb Version

C#9

AH, EV - 'RY TEAR THAT I'VE CRIED _____

B9   F#9   F#9/A#   B9   C°7

ON-LY WASHED A-WAY THE FEAR IN - SIDE. __ NOW I, _____   I AIN'T GONE 'N' GIVE UP ON _____

BRIDGE

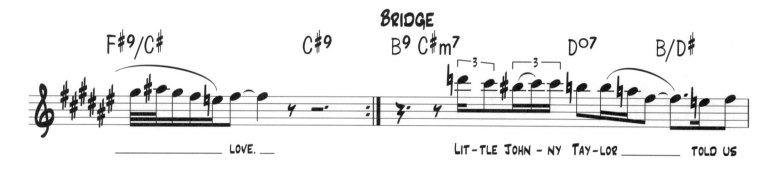

F#9/C#   C#9   B9   C#m7   D°7   B/D#

_____ LOVE. ___   LIT-TLE JOHN - NY TAY-LOR _____ TOLD US

F#9 G#m7   A°7   F#/A#   B   C#m7   D°7   B/D#

SO __ LONG __ A - GO ___   ALL A-BOUT __ THE MID-NIGHT CRY - IN'.

F#9 G#m7   A°7   F#/A#   B9   C#m7   D°7   B/D#

WHOA, __ 'N' THAT YOU BEEN LY-IN'.   WHAT A-BOUT THE PRICE ___ THAT WILL, __

F#9 G#m7   A°7   F#/A#   G#7   A#m7   B°7   G#/B#

OH, ___ SURE-LY BE PAID _____   'CAUSE THEY GAVE UP ON LOVE?

Love will ___ have its day. _____ I ain't ___ giv-in' up on ____

Solos

_____ love. ___

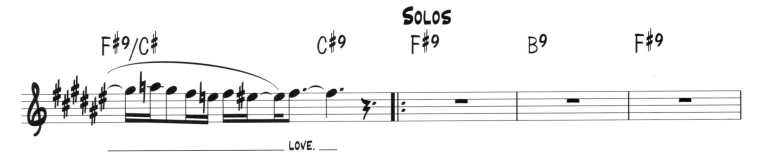

Outro-Verse

3. I ain't gon' give up on ___ love. ___ Love _____ won't give up

on ___ me. _____

I __ AIN'T GONE 'N' GIVE UP ON _____ LOVE. __

__ LOVE, _____ WON'T GIVE, AH. UP ON __ ME, _____ AH, HA. __

__ EV - 'RY TIME __ I CRY, _____

LORD, __ JUST, AH, WON'T 'N' LET __ ME, __ ME __ BE. _____

SLIGHT RIT.

ADDITIONAL LYRICS

2. EV'RY BEAT OF MY HEART POUNDS WITH JOY 'N' NOT PAIN.
   EV'RY BEAT OF MY HEART POUNDS WITH JOY 'N' BURNIN' PAIN.
   'CAUSE ALL THOSE PAINFUL MEMORIES ONLY BROUGHT ME TO MY KNEES.
   I WAS JUST GIVIN' UP ON LOVE.

Couldn't Stand the Weather

Written by Stevie Ray Vaughan

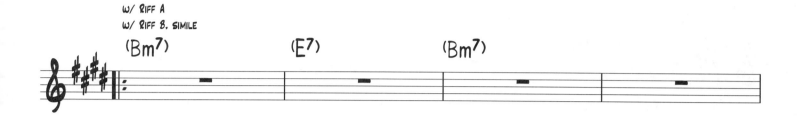

w/ Riff A
w/ Riff B, simile

VERSE

Bm⁷

1. Com - in' through ___ this a bus-'ness of life, ___
2. *See additional lyrics*

Rare - ly time ___ if I'm need - ed to. ___

Ain't so fun - ny when things ___ ain't feel - in' right, ___

THEN DAD-DY'S HAND ___ HELPS TO SEE ME THROUGH. ___

G#m

SWEET AS SUG-AR, LOVE WON'T ___ WASH A-WAY. ___ F#7 RAIN OR SHINE, IT'S AL-

E7

- WAYS HERE TO STAY. ___ ALL THESE YEARS, YOU 'N' I'VE

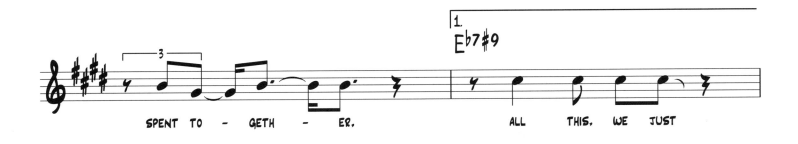

1.
Eb7#9

SPENT TO-GETH-ER, ALL THIS, WE JUST

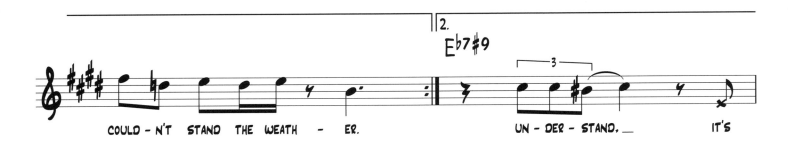

2.
Eb7#9

COULD-N'T STAND THE WEATH-ER. UN-DER-STAND, ___ IT'S

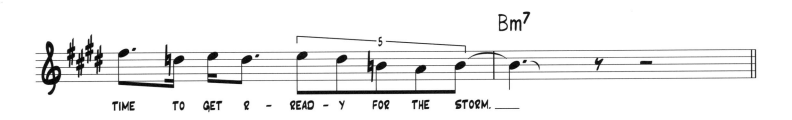

Bm7

TIME TO GET R-READ-Y FOR THE STORM. ___

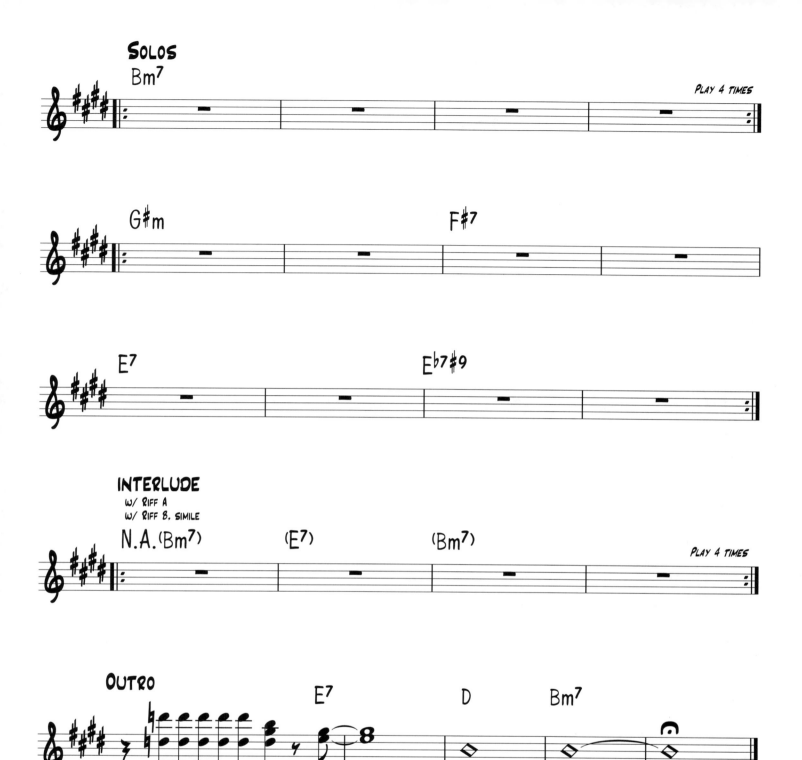

Additional Lyrics

2. Like a train that stops at ev'ry station,
   We all deal with trials and tribulations.
   Fear hangs the fellow that ties up his years,
   Entangled in yellow and cries all his tears.
   Changes come before we can go.
   Learn to see them before we're too old.
   Don't just take me for tryin' to be heavy.
   Understand, it's time to get ready for the storm.

Crossfire

Words and Music by Bill Carter, Ruth Ellsworth, Reese Wynans, Tommy Shannon and Chris Layton

Eb Version

CAUGHT IN ___ THE CROSS - FIRE.

STRAND - ED, _____
{ 2. I AM STRAND - ED, _____ }
{ 3. WE GOT STRAND - ED, _____ }

BRIDGE
E7

CAUGHT IN THE CROSS - FIRE.   I NEED SOME

F#7   E7   F#7

KIND OF KIND - NESS, __   SOME KIND OF SYM - PA - THY. ___ OH,   NO, ___   WE'RE

N.C.(C#7)

STRAND - ED, ___   CAUGHT IN THE CROSS - FIRE.

SOLOS
C#7   Play 4 times   E7

F#7   E7   F#7   C#

D.S. al Coda

Coda

CAUGHT IN THE CROSS-

- FIRE. WE GOT STRAND - ED, _____

CAUGHT IN THE CROSS - FIRE. STRAND - ED, _____

CAUGHT IN _____ THE CROSS - FIRE.

Outro-Solo

C#7

Play 7 times

N.C. C#7#9

Additional Lyrics

2. Tooth for tooth, eye for an eye,
   Sell your soul just to buy, buy, buy.
   Beggin' a dollar, steal-in' a dime,
   Come on, can't cha see that I,...

3. Save the strong, lose the weak,
   Never turning the other cheek.
   Trust nobody, don't be no fool.
   Whatever happened to the golden rule?

Honey Bee

Written by Stevie Ray Vaughan

Eb Version

Don't make me wait to feel your warm em-brace.

Each and ev-'ry time that we get the chance, __ C-

G#7   C#7   To Coda ⊕

'mon, lit-tle ba-by, let's, ah, make some ro - mance.

Solo
C#7

F#7   C#7

G#7   F#7   C#7

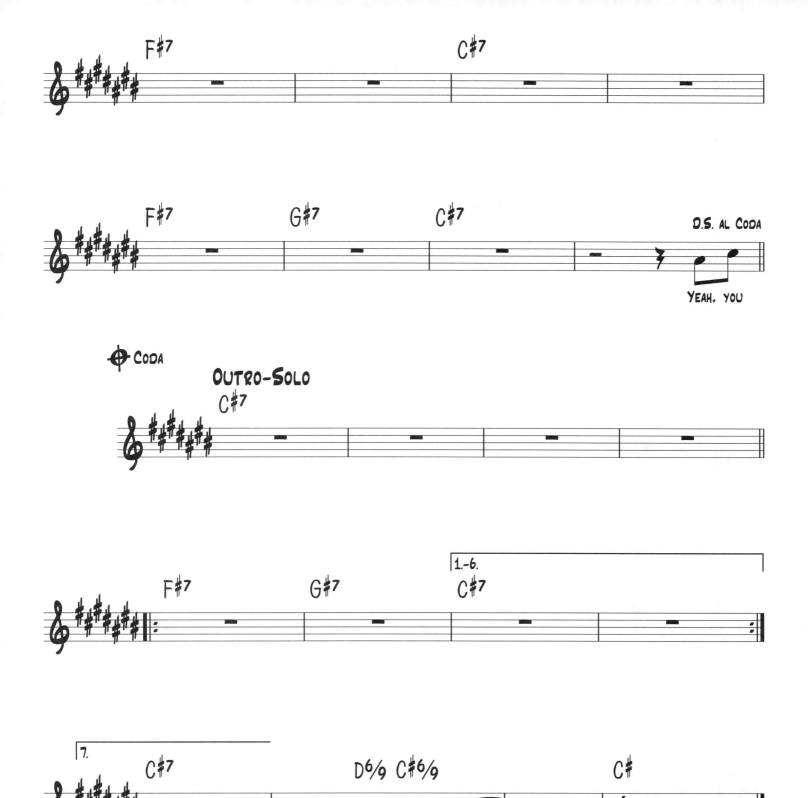

ADDITIONAL LYRICS

Bridge: YEAH, YOU REALLY GROOVE ME, BABY, WHEN YOU MOVE YOUR HIPS.
SHAKE IT ALL AROUND, IT TAKES ME POUND FOR POUND.
I WANT YOU ALL THE TIME JUST BECAUSE,
YOU KNOW YOU REALLY HAVE GIVE ME A BUZZ.

Empty Arms

Written by Stevie Ray Vaughan

Eb Version

Intro
Moderately fast ♩ = 142

Band enters

Intro/Solo

1. YOU'RE GON - NA MISS __

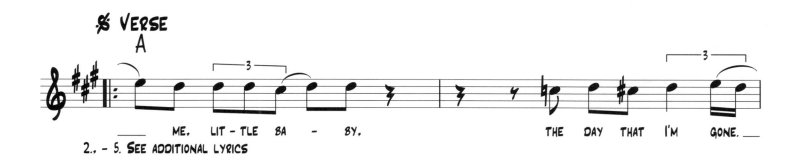

%. VERSE
A

__ ME, LIT - TLE BA - BY, THE DAY THAT I'M GONE. __

2., - 5. SEE ADDITIONAL LYRICS

You're gon - na miss ___ me, lit - tle dar - lin',

the day that I'm gone. ___ 'Cause I'm

5th time, to Coda

Leav - in' in the morn - in', won't be back at all. ___

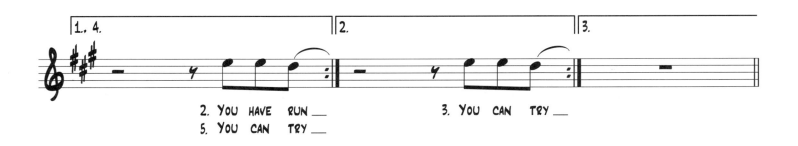

1. 4.
2. You have run ___
5. You can try ___

2.
3. You can try ___

3.

Solos
A

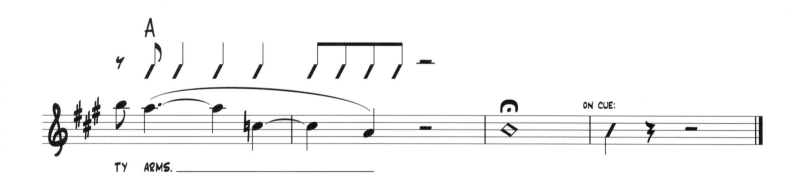

Additional Lyrics

2., 4. You have run me ragged, baby,
It's your own fault you're on your own.
You have run me ragged, darlin',
It's your own fault you're on your own.
You didn't want me to wait, baby,
Till your other man was gone.

3., 5. You can try to ge me back, baby,
With all your tricks and charms.
You can try to get me back, baby,
With all your tricks and charms.
But when all your games are over,
You'll be left with empty arms.

Rude Mood

Written by Stevie Ray Vaughan

Eb Version

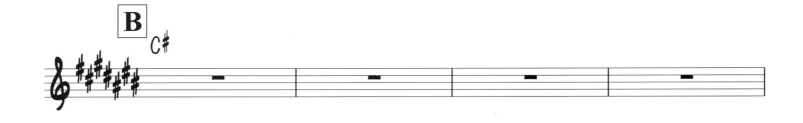

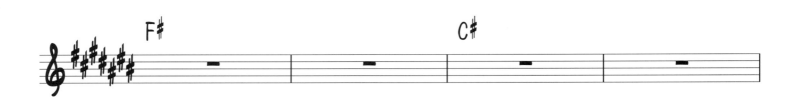

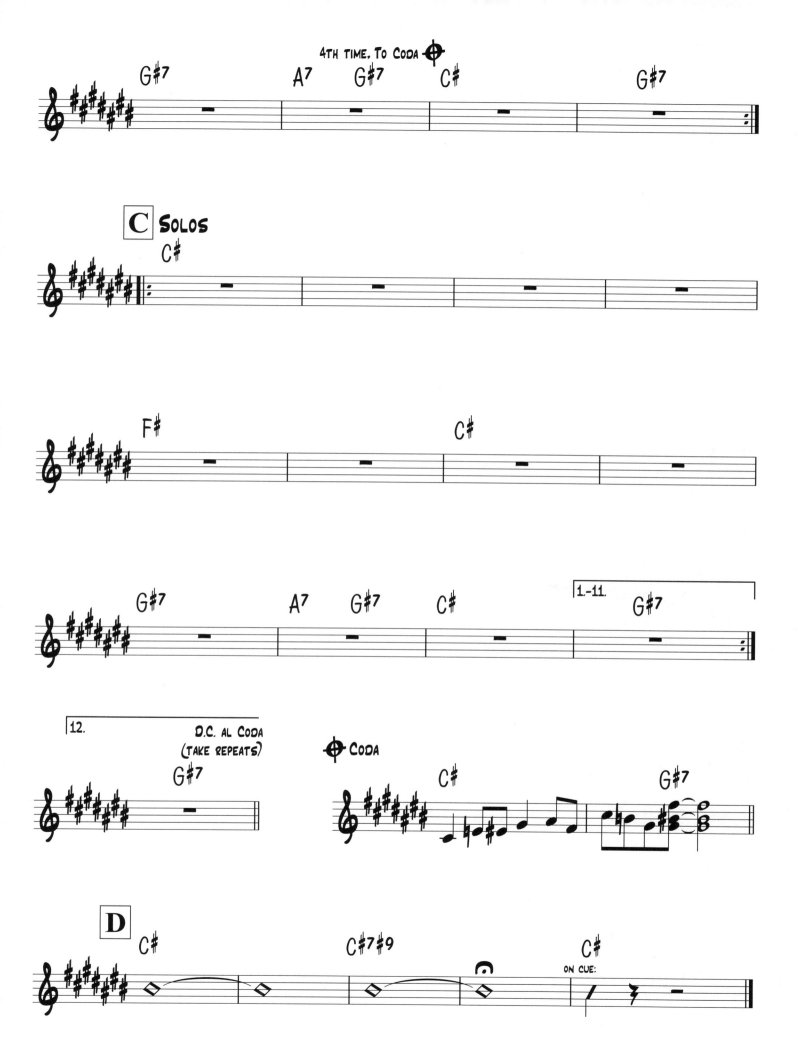

Scuttle Buttin'

Written by Stevie Ray Vaughan

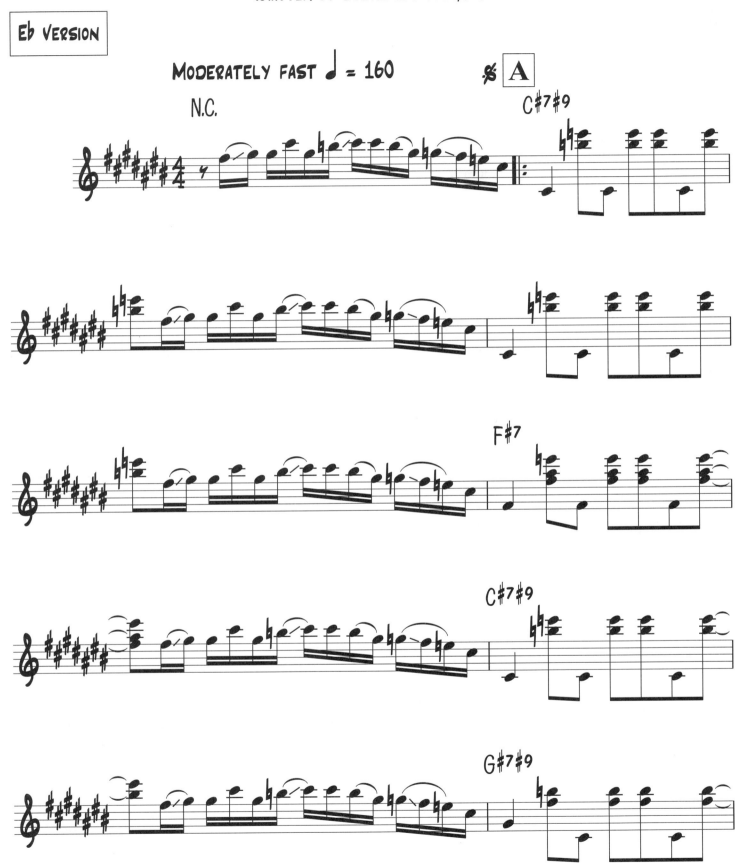

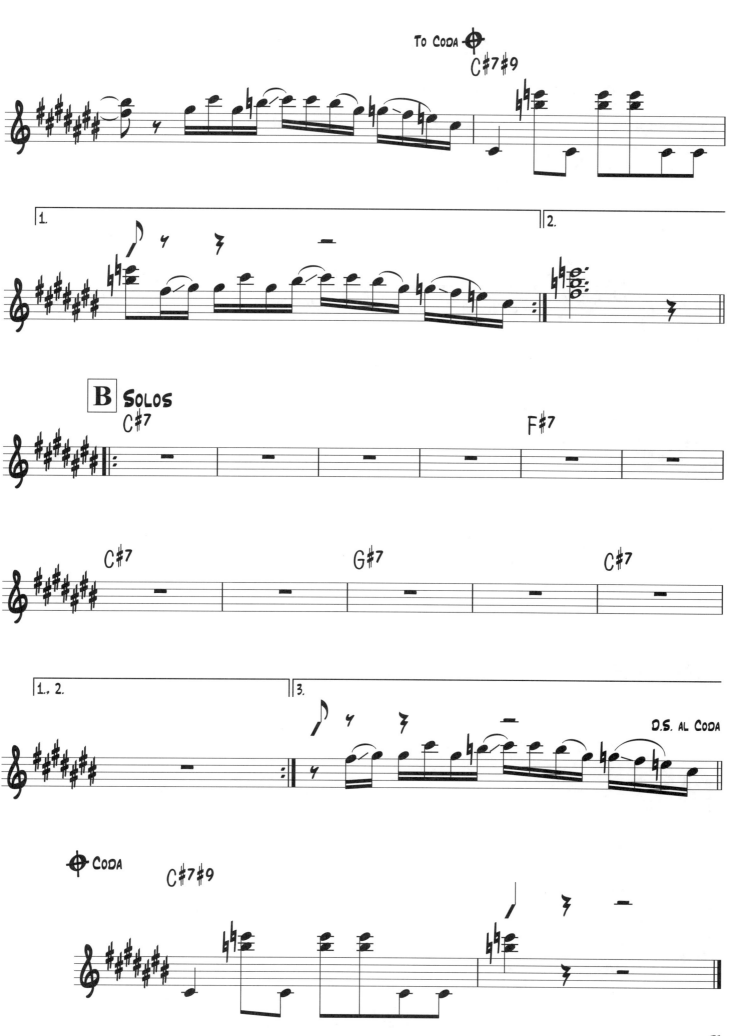

Love Struck Baby

Written by Stevie Ray Vaughan

Eb Version

LOVE YOU, BA - BY, AN' I KNOW JUST WHAT TO DO. _____

%. VERSE

1. I _____ STILL RE - MEM BER, AN' LET IT BE SAID. _____ THE
2., 3. *SEE ADDITIONAL LYRICS*

WAY YOU MAKE ME FEEL, IT'LL TAKE A FOOL TO FOR - GET. I SWORE A TON OF BRICKS HAD HIT ME

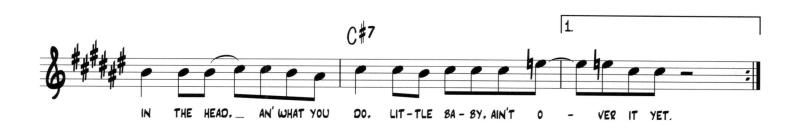

IN THE HEAD, _ AN' WHAT YOU DO, LIT-TLE BA - BY, AIN'T O - VER IT YET.

CHORUS

_____ YOUR MAN? I'M A LOVE STRUCK, BA - BY. YEAH, I'M A

LOVE STRUCK, BA - BY. YOU GOT ME LOVE STRUCK, BA - BY,

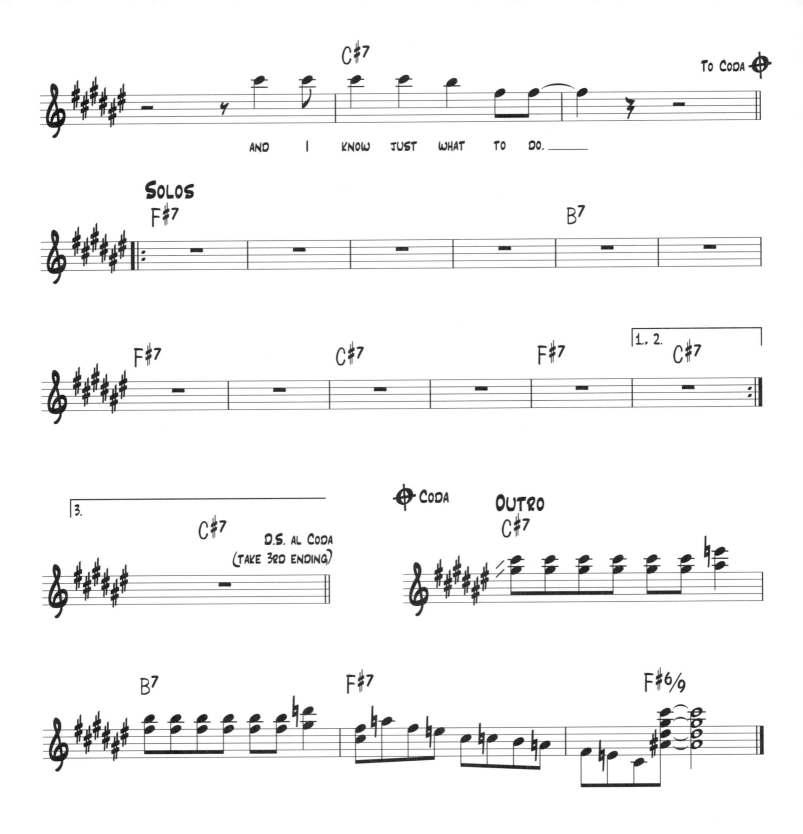

Additional Lyrics

2. Everytime I see you, make me feel so fine.
   Heart beatin' crazy, my blood runnin' wild.
   Lovin' makes me feel like a mighty, mighty man.
   Love me, baby, ain't I your man?

3. Sparks start flyin' everytime we meet.
   Let me tell you, baby, you knock me off my feet.
   Your kisses trip me up and they're just dog gone sweet.
   Don't you know, baby, you knock me off my feet?

Crossfire

Words and Music by Bill Carter, Ruth Ellsworth, Reese Wynans, Tommy Shannon and Chris Layton

OUTRO-SOLO

E⁷

Play 7 times

N.C.   E⁷♯9

ADDITIONAL LYRICS

2. TOOTH FOR TOOTH, EYE FOR AN EYE,
   SELL YOUR SOUL JUST TO BUY, BUY, BUY.
   BEGGIN' A DOLLAR, STEAL-IN' A DIME,
   COME ON, CAN'T CHA SEE THAT I,...

3. SAVE THE STRONG, LOSE THE WEAK,
   NEVER TURNING THE OTHER CHEEK.
   TRUST NOBODY, DON'T BE NO FOOL.
   WHATEVER HAPPENED TO THE GOLDEN RULE?

Ain't Gone 'N' Give Up On Love

Written by Stevie Ray Vaughan

AH, EV - 'RY TEAR THAT I'VE CRIED

ON-LY WASHED A-WAY THE FEAR IN - SIDE. __ NOW I, _____ I AIN'T GONE 'N' GIVE UP ON _____

BRIDGE

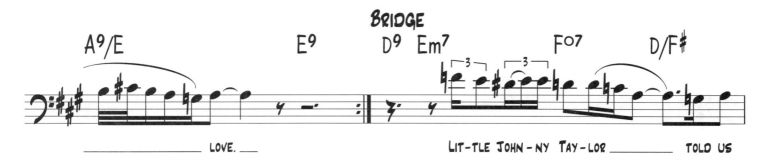

LOVE. ___ LIT-TLE JOHN-NY TAY-LOR _____ TOLD US

SO ___ LONG ___ A-GO ___ ALL A-BOUT __ THE MID-NIGHT CRY - IN',

WHOA, __ 'N' THAT YOU BEEN LY-IN'. WHAT A-BOUT THE PRICE ___ THAT WILL, __

OH, ___ SURE - LY BE PAID _____ 'CAUSE THEY GAVE UP ON LOVE?

Love will _ have its day. _____ I ain't   giv-in' up on _____

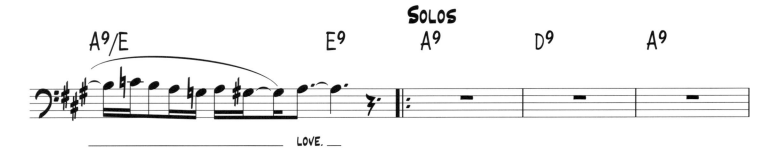

SOLOS

_____ Love. _

OUTRO-VERSE

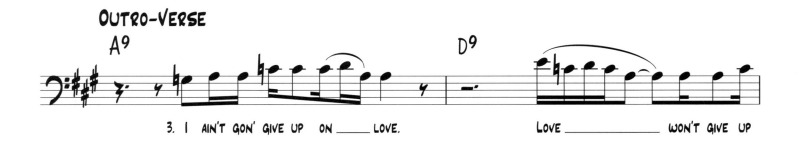

3. I ain't gon' give up on _____ love.   Love _____ won't give up

On _____ me. _____

I AIN'T GONE 'N' GIVE UP ON _____ LOVE.

_____ LOVE, _____ WON'T GIVE, AH, UP ON ___ ME, _____ AH, HA. ___

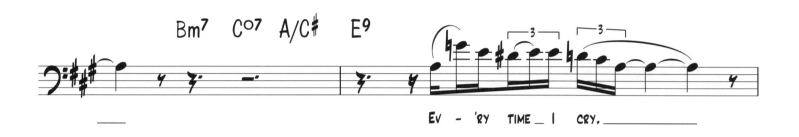

EV - 'RY TIME __ I CRY, _____

LORD, __ JUST, AH, WON'T 'N' LET __ ME, ___ ME __ BE. _____

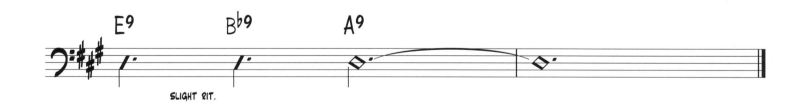

SLIGHT RIT.

ADDITIONAL LYRICS

2. Ev'ry beat of my heart pounds with joy 'n' not pain.
   Ev'ry beat of my heart pounds with joy 'n' burnin' pain.
   'Cause all those painful memories only brought me to my knees.
   I was just givin' up on love.

Couldn't Stand the Weather

Written by Stevie Ray Vaughan

(Dm⁷)

w/ Riff A
w/ Riff B, simile

(Dm⁷)   (G⁷)   (Dm⁷)

(G⁷)   (Dm⁷)

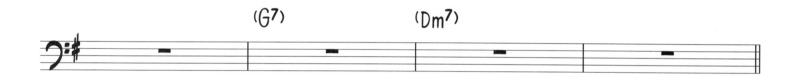

VERSE
Dm⁷

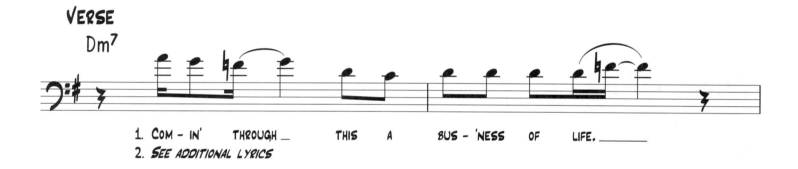

1. COM - IN' THROUGH __ THIS A BUS - 'NESS OF LIFE, ____
2. *SEE ADDITIONAL LYRICS*

RARE - LY TIME ___ IF I'M NEED - ED TO. _____

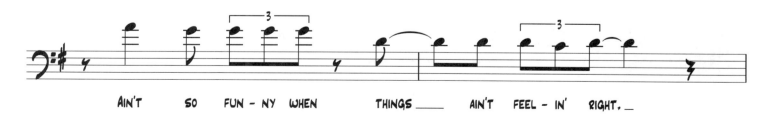

AIN'T SO FUN - NY WHEN THINGS ____ AIN'T FEEL - IN' RIGHT, __

THEN DAD-DY'S HAND __ HELPS TO SEE ME THROUGH. __

Bm

SWEET AS SUG-AR, LOVE WON'T __ WASH A-WAY. __ RAIN OR SHINE, IT'S AL -

A7

G7

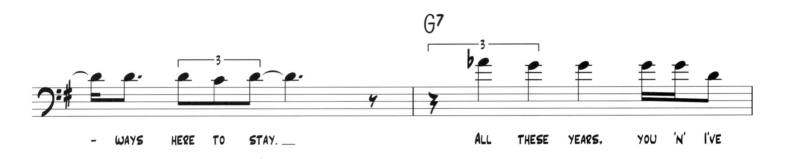

- WAYS HERE TO STAY. __ ALL THESE YEARS, YOU 'N' I'VE

1.
F#7#9

SPENT TO - GETH - ER. ALL THIS, WE JUST

2.
F#7#9

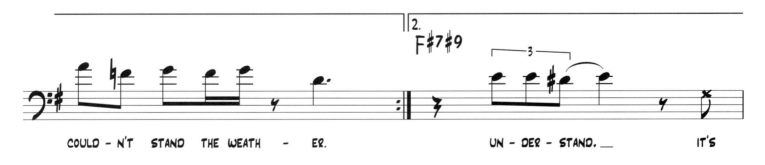

COULD - N'T STAND THE WEATH - ER. UN - DER - STAND, __ IT'S

Dm7

TIME TO GET R - READ-Y FOR THE STORM. ___

ADDITIONAL LYRICS

2. Like a train that stops at ev'ry station,
We all deal with trials and tribulations.
Fear hangs the fellow that ties up his years,
Entangled in yellow and cries all his tears.
Changes come before we can go.
Learn to see them before we're too old.
Don't just take me for tryin' to be heavy.
Understand, it's time to get ready for the storm.

Empty Arms

Written by Stevie Ray Vaughan

 C Version

Intro

Moderately fast ♩ = 142

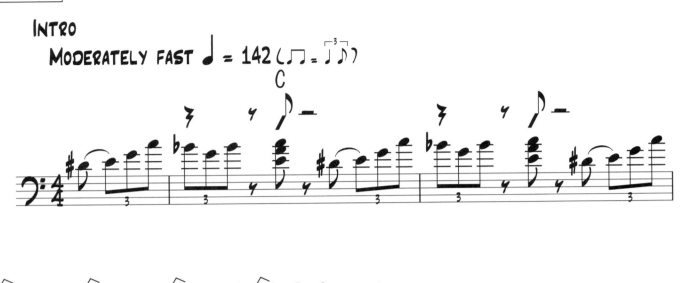

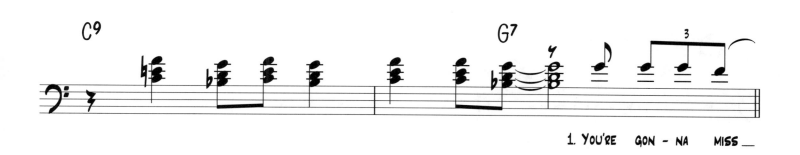

1. YOU'RE GON - NA MISS __

𝄋 VERSE

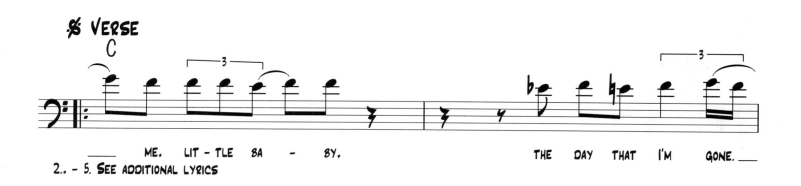

__ ME, LIT - TLE BA - BY, THE DAY THAT I'M GONE. __

2., - 5. SEE ADDITIONAL LYRICS

YOU'RE GON-NA MISS ___ ME, LIT-TLE DAR - LIN',

THE DAY THAT I'M GONE. _____ 'CAUSE I'M

LEAV-IN' IN THE MORN - IN', WON'T BE BACK AT ALL. _____

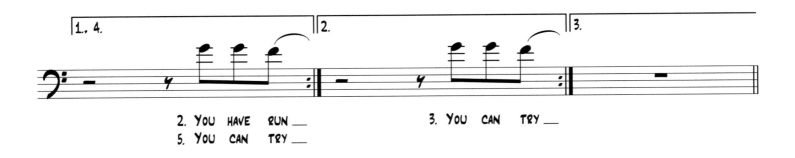

2. YOU HAVE RUN ___
5. YOU CAN TRY ___

3. YOU CAN TRY ___

SOLOS

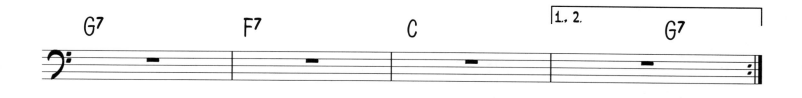

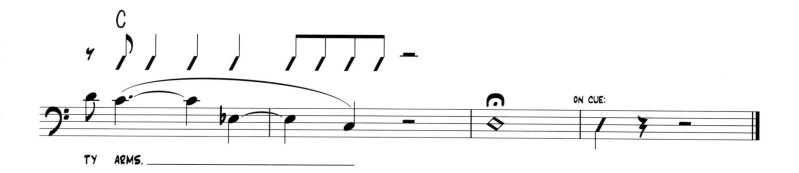

ADDITIONAL LYRICS

2., 4. YOU HAVE RUN ME RAGGED, BABY,
IT'S YOUR OWN FAULT YOU'RE ON YOUR OWN.
YOU HAVE RUN ME RAGGED, DARLIN'.
IT'S YOUR OWN FAULT YOU'RE ON YOUR OWN.
YOU DIDN'T WANT ME TO WAIT, BABY,
TILL YOUR OTHER MAN WAS GONE.

3., 5. YOU CAN TRY TO GE ME BACK, BABY,
WITH ALL YOUR TRICKS AND CHARMS.
YOU CAN TRY TO GET ME BACK, BABY,
WITH ALL YOUR TRICKS AND CHARMS.
BUT WHEN ALL YOUR GAMES ARE OVER,
YOU'LL BE LEFT WITH EMPTY ARMS.

Honey Bee

Written by Stevie Ray Vaughan

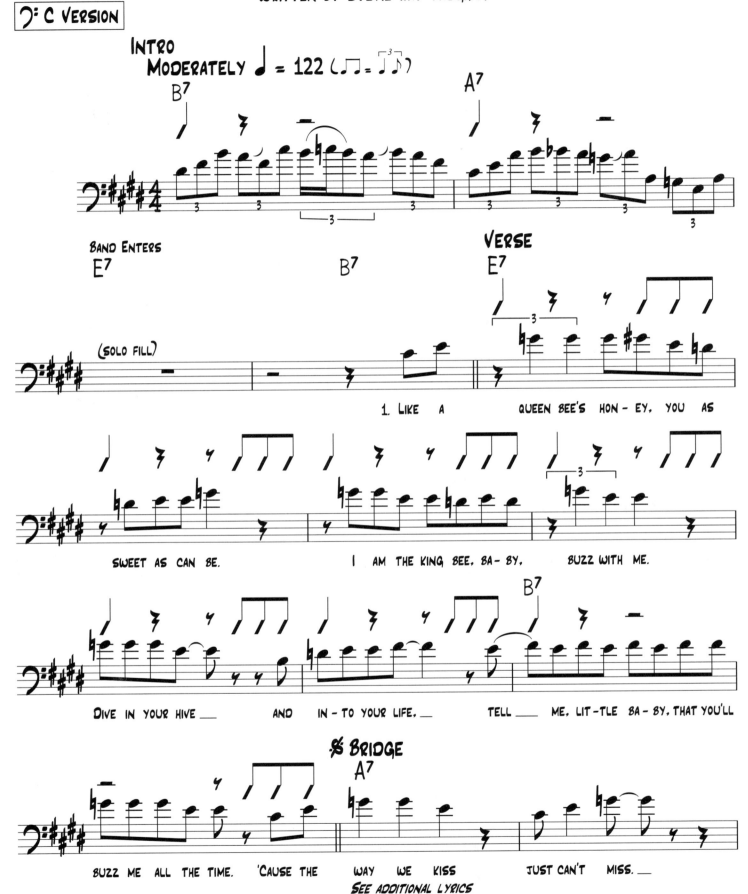

Don't make me wait to feel your warm em - brace.

Each and ev - 'ry time that we get the chance, __ c -

B⁷   E⁷   To Coda ⊕

'mon, lit - tle ba - by, let's, ah, make some ro - mance.

Solo

E⁷

A⁷   E⁷

B⁷   A⁷   E⁷

D.S. al Coda

Yeah, you

⊕ **Coda**

Outro-Solo

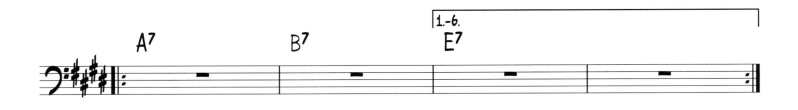

1.-6.

7.

Additional Lyrics

Bridge: Yeah, you really groove me, baby, when you move your hips.
Shake it all around, it takes me pound for pound.
I want you all the time just because,
You know you really have give me a buzz.

Love Struck Baby

Written by Stevie Ray Vaughan

LOVE YOU, BA - BY, AN' I KNOW JUST WHAT TO DO. ___

%. VERSE

1. I ___ STILL RE - MEM - BER, AN' LET IT BE SAID, ___ THE
2., 3. *SEE ADDITIONAL LYRICS*

WAY YOU MAKE ME FEEL, IT'LL TAKE A FOOL TO FOR - GET. I SWORE A TON OF BRICKS HAD HIT ME

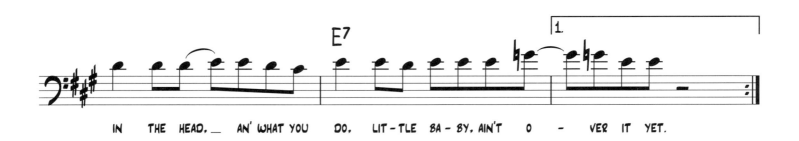

IN THE HEAD, ___ AN' WHAT YOU DO, LIT - TLE BA - BY, AIN'T O - VER IT YET.

CHORUS

___ YOUR MAN? I'M A LOVE STRUCK, BA - BY. YEAH, I'M A

LOVE STRUCK, BA - BY. YOU GOT ME LOVE STRUCK, BA - BY,

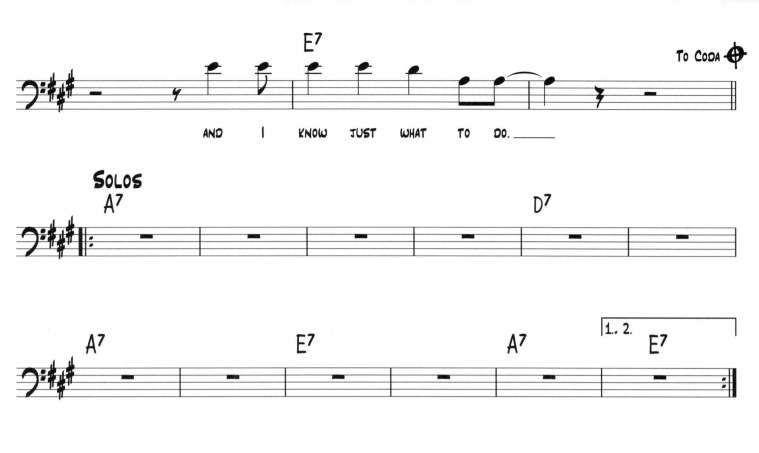

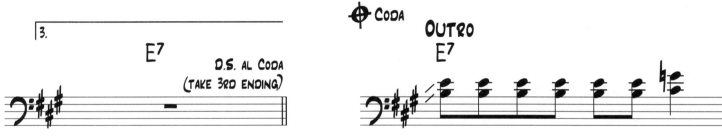

Additional Lyrics

2. Everytime I see you, make me feel so fine.
   Heart beatin' crazy, my blood runnin' wild.
   Lovin' makes me feel like a mighty, mighty man.
   Love me, baby, ain't I your man?

3. Sparks start flyin' everytime we meet.
   Let me tell you, baby, you knock me off my feet.
   Your kisses trip me up and they're just dog gone sweet.
   Don't you know, baby, you knock me off my feet?

Rude Mood

Written by Stevie Ray Vaughan

🎼 C Version

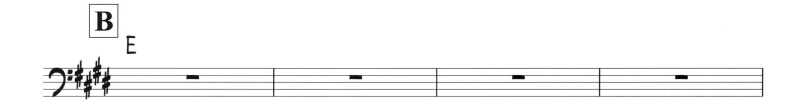

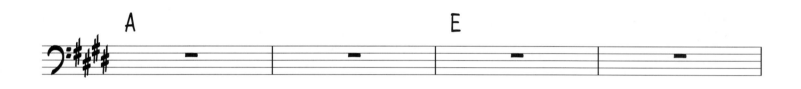

Scuttle Buttin'

Written by Stevie Ray Vaughan

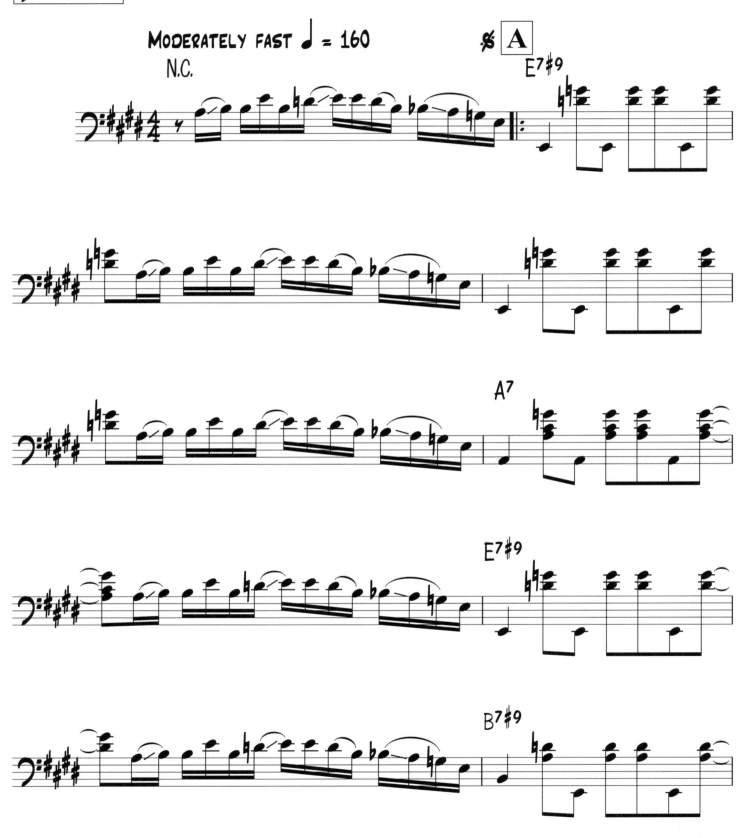

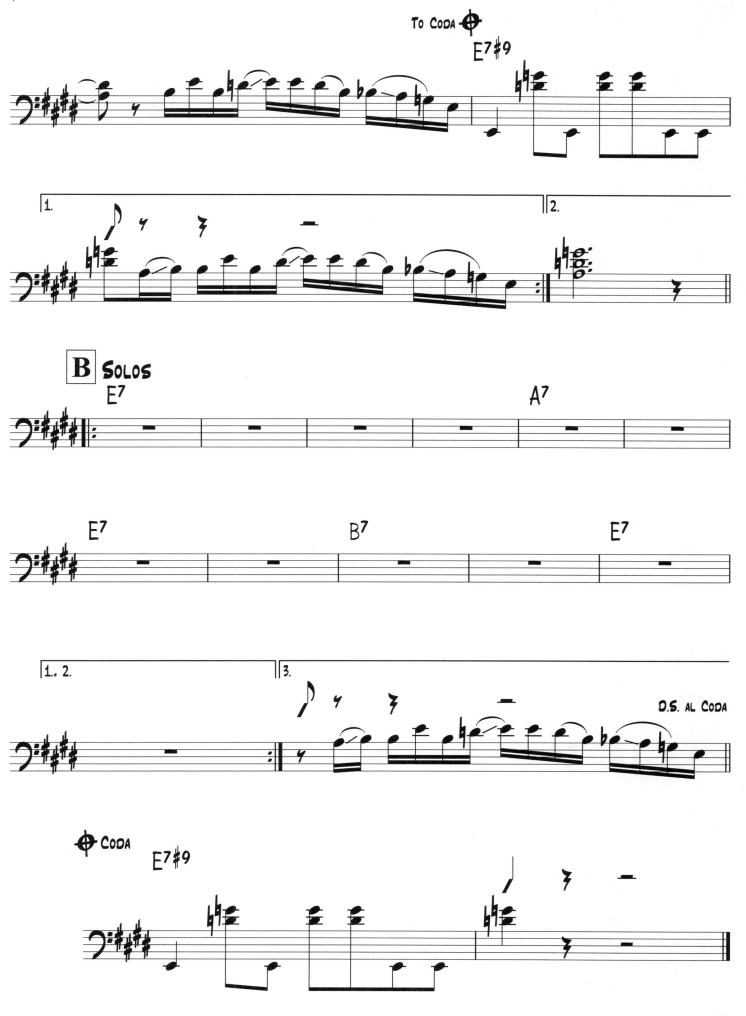